T0162043

THE DRUG OF CHOICE

CHRISTOPHER CAHILL   THE DRUG OF CHOICE

TURTLE POINT PRESS NEW YORK

PUBLISHED BY TURTLE POINT PRESS

WWW.TURTLEPOINTPRESS.COM

COPYRIGHT © 2012 BY CHRISTOPHER CAHILL

ALL RIGHTS RESERVED

ISBN 978-1-933527-64-2

LCCN 2012934895

DESIGN AND COMPOSITION BY QUEMADURA

PRINTED ON ACID-FREE, RECYCLED PAPER

IN THE UNITED STATES OF AMERICA

TO LIZZIE

I

I

LAMPLIGHTING

The curfew tolls the death of Little Nell.
Nearby a dog barks at a rival dog
barking nearby, and if not for these alarms
there would be more to call us out from thought,
from work, the eyes desperate to rest
against the blue evening air we missed
the onslaught of, stars in place
before the ink has dried, urging us
to kill the lights and let the night take hold
of us along with the museum's battlements,
the trees' branches rooted in the sky,
the lonely passengers drifting home
after one more day of unrecorded longing.

The message of the night is simple and familiar.
The moon spells it out in marble hieroglyphs.
It is asking us to recollect the love
made, by us as well, on beds and couches
spaced throughout the empty house.
It is letting us know how soon that vanishes,
how quick the come dries on the flesh
she wiped it on that once, then flakes away,
words we thought had meaning gone
the unremembered way of words.

Tonight Nell dies again, it says, little or not,
attended by her dying father, attending him,

he dies. The heart of stone laughs, cries,
stops and is forgotten. Out in the air
a colorless wind is rubbing its eraser
slowly over the visible world.
Nothing seems to vanish but it does.

A MISREADING OF CARAVAGGIO'S

CRUCIFIXION OF SAINT PETER

The first thing you notice is that he's older
than you'd thought. His beard is white,
the hair's gone bald on the crown of his head
and he has a thick set of muscles straining
away at the ropes as he worries how he's going
to get out of this one. More than anything
he looks like a weatherbeaten sea captain who's lost
this time and is on the verge
of getting tossed overboard
by the pirates.

Then there are the three guidos busy with the bully work
though they don't seem to be making
much of a job of it.
One of them's squatting braced up
against the underside of the cross
like he's playing Johnny-Ride-the-Pony
and he's pushing the cross *up*
upside downwards and he has a shovel
in his hands as though he's missing the whole
point of the occasion. The other two
seem equally inept or at cross purposes
to the story and he's made it
night even though it was late morning.

For all its mistakes, though, it's an unsettling vision.
There's the dirt on the bottom of the one guy's
bare feet and there's his pants like a wet chamois
and how their faces are hidden in shadow
or turned away so that they remind you
of real Romans of the kind
who would beat you up and rob you outside
of the hideous train station after
you've wandered off down the wrong
sidestreet looking for a bite to eat.
And there's the way you don't realize at first
with the murk that the nails are in there already
though they haven't been pounded down —

it makes you think there must be another one
of them holding the hammer just off to the right of the frame
who's bossing these others around and telling them
what a bunch of fuckups they are.
He'd have his name in the Bible, that one,
they all would, though it's strange we don't know them
as anything but soldiers and you have to admire
the way Caravaggio has pictured them
like extras from *The Valachi Papers* trying
to sink some squealer into the Gowanus Canal.

These are the soldiers, then,
and the one they have down
there and are getting ready to go
at with the hammer and nails,
that would be Jesus, ignorant

of all his sacred name would swell to and command
after his death, scared now and ready
to admit if it would save him that he believes
in the usual lineup of gods
and to praise them where they are, spread out across the sky
as stars that just happen to be hidden
by the afternoon light.

CONTRA NATURAM

So why do you cry out to nature now who never
loved you and lets the wild vine rise
as though a charmer's music led it
upwards, cantilevered against walls of air,
while your own breath falls short and goes
unnoticed in its failing? You're not to be
heard, so why speak pointlessly into
the moist sprung light of another day
you won't, at its end, consider your own?

You want the world to admire how you've grown,
to promise to love, honor, and obey
its loveless once-beloved child, don't you?
Watch. A bee drones and drops lightly
over spent blossoms ruinous
and placid in their disrepair.
The world is shit.
Mourn that, if you like, and despise
the fall that follows, without you, therever.

THE SAGE OF WEST END AVENUE

I used to say these things
and to others, no less,
like how, with bums,
I would always answer
them, saying no
I couldn't spare
the change, just so
they wouldn't think
they weren't human
in my eyes.

I haven't acknowledged
a bum in years
and wonder what's become
of my wisdom.
Not sleeping, I've grown
scatterbrained and lack
what my old gym teacher
would call follow-through.
When someone else's roof
falls from under

my feet I'll be out
with them, ignoring
my own pleas for help.
For the meanwhile I try
to give advice while I

have some still. My brother,
I told him never to
fall for barmaids—
it's their job
to smile at you.

1979

I'm standing idly by while Denis
or "Dino" McCarney (him of the wire-rimmed specs
and the hair like a set of loosening springs)
unzips his army pants, extracts his penis,
and pisses stoutly into Chuck Gilvary's brown quart bottle of flattening
Bud. He sleeps for now but soon will wake and drink. I've only just had sex

of a kind with Marina Moran in the convent
doorway of our alma ma'
and am still adhesive with the dried distillate.
Magnolias have blossomed here with their smell of unripened melons.
I'm licking each finger of my right
hand, drunk in the park with these fledgling felons.
By now she's home at her parents' second apartment
brushing her braceless teeth, stripped of her training bra.

II. MT. SINAI

Unless that was the night when the Fungus
Brothers flipped onto one of the quartzite
chess tables three bags of a cocaine so crosscut
and stepped on that it found, among the connoisseurs,
no takers; the very night
I waited in the back seat of a hand-shammied bootblack Duster
with Joey Ona and Brian Dane, each of us
set after this girl with a body like a bowlful of tit

who was inside visiting her cancerous or, maybe, car-wrecked
uncle. We'd picked up her and her ugly
friend at Mimi's. I was turning over in my mind
an image I had recently purloined
from *The Year of the French*. The bright black hood reflected
the unblinking neon word EMERGENCY.

III. 84TH AND YORK

And then I said nothing
as this chimp-faced Bowery Boy with a homemade blood
blue tattoo of a cross on the back of his hand
three times touched the tip of a cigarette to the polyester blend
windbreaker Stephanie Myles wore knotted
around her ample waist. And then I stood

by. In the parish of St. Stephen of Hungary.
Stephanie Myles and her friend Irene—
feathered hair, tight white pants, eyeshadow blue as a morpho's wing
and dusty—a pretty guttertongue
who'd been raped summerlong
by her rusticated uncle and cousin
and had returned to the city
prepared to fuck anything.

IV. PIER 74

But enough about all that, enough
already. I'd rather fix my mind's eye on
a potted fern hung in smoke and breath
above the bar at Cobblestones (formerly Carroll's),
on the crazed shadow it gives across the skin
of Jill Hellman, leaning close to hear me, and her tough
but gorgeous friend Deirdre Down, the youngest of six girls,
six beauties who have spent the '70s as a sort of private bakery of love and death

so steady is their transit between conception and abortion.
This pair have just come from Studio 54 or The Mint.
I'm too hammered to make the connection.
In the morning I'll meet Lenny B. at the Hudson River helipad,
looking like I've downed a thousand pints of lint,
then catch a ride to the beach with Mom and Dad.

That you've got to go down
on a lobster is one thing he taught me that afternoon—
the emptied shells on the garden table so clean and filled with light
when he was done
with them the small vaults of the buttery white
interiors glowed red as the tortured defunct exoskeletons—

that you should go down on all things living and desired.
The 3rd of July. His face ashine
from what he'd pushed it into. Ebony and ivory; an opera
of *Lolita*; Humbert Humbert singing "Hey Big Daddy
you're making me batty"—
he'd put that one aside but would try it again if I'd
do the libretto. Would I? Lust, I guess. Life. I'm taking it all as *opera buffa*.
I have my eye fixed on some distant mine.

NYC

Granite reef on which I've been a minnow
these forty years,
never growing as you've died
and risen
more than once, threading the tides
of tar, trees, cars,
dogshit, citizens, and strangers, I owe

you all the money in my pockets, not
a lot, I know,
but what I have to keep me
here. Chosen
city, unregal city,
city of low
lifes and loveless sex, of cigars put out

on flesh for pleasure—absolute power
absolutely
corrupts you and the shadow
knows what lurks
behind the penthouse window,
the cold, filthy
ghetto basement grate where creatures lower

than the shar-pei and the Siamese cat
work at sewing
machines and electric looms,
aging young.
For years I've moved through your dreams,
never knowing
when you'd wake and I'd be gone, slingshot out

into America with the armies
of cabdrivers,
cops, communists, prostitutes,
bums, well-hung
callboys, repairers of lutes,
scubadivers,
muffdivers, rabbinical scholars, cheese-

shop owners, barmaids, forgers, simpletons
and masterminds,
Italians, Kurds, Phoenicians,
Chinese, Turks,
Irish, WASPs, Dominicans—
the undesigned
superfluousness of generation

that clogs the narrow streets of your islands
with its bodies
unfit for life on the plains,
the lonely
open land that bears the stains
so visibly
of each human passage through its silence.

Here if you incinerate your parents'
Village townhouse
with a misfired shrapnel bomb
the only
sign left soon will be the calm,
odd quietus
imposed upon the nearby apartments

in the long aftermath; here the chorus
of birdspeech hides
its tuneless notes in the far
off reaches
of the North Woods, Central Park,
and the time slides
by when echoes from the heart's own forest

might be given rise to and become song;
here the last light
spreads its legs for those high up
enough to
sit by cleaned windows and sip
the coming night,
set with stars, tiny cubes of ice the lungs

are glad of as the eyes warm to the pale
blue rosecolored
fleshy aetherial show
the bought view
affords; here those in the know
have discovered
the key to suffering in comfort, fail

as they will to dodge the great hand that sweeps
us all aside
like white sand blown light along
the beaches
of Brooklyn, Queens, and my Long
Island, the wide
precincts where time and again the mind keeps

turning, presage of its long extinction;
here the hot air
in summer is wet as hot
dog water
and those days and nights are shot
through with the bare
desire for sex, the avid secretion

of self onto life — which won't come again,
unless I'm wrong;
here the winter bites its tongue,
spring flatters
the common breath with each lung-
ful of its strong
perfume, and fall shines dark with beetled rain;

there's a there here and a now too, but there's
barely a then,
though, barely a then. Who'll know,
in the end,
that the chiaroscuro
of a certain
stumbledrunken morning sidewalk — its glares

and glass, its unglown, on-kilter bars
and blocks and spines
of shadow, its unfailing
rectitude
of shape and mass, its falling
bar-graph of lines
strung tight as tungsten—that all this—hard scars

and luminance—lasts and then stopped lasting,
that the past here
goes on a while once it's gone
and then goes
for good. Who'll know that what shone,
or seemed to, there,
was dead by then past all trial or testing.

From my balcony I watch a red-tailed
hawk volte and beck
in the half-bright field of air
suspended
for his play between the clear
sky and bedrock,
diamondheaded mote of the fascicled

towers, from whom the pigeons scatter as
one, as though swung
in a great transparent net—
oilslicked, crude-
crayoned neck-feathers sunset-
lit but unsung
still; aerial ratpack; ringwormed chorus—

and as they wheel behind him, white-panached
wingbacks crescent
in shine, his fanned tail takes sun,
shimmers, glows
palpebrally, an eon-
fed full instant
so wrapped up in its now that no vanished

hour seems feasible, so submerged in things-
as-they-are-al-
ways you can almost believe
what matters
is not the next kill, the grief
to come, but all
this air, the poised, upheld, unbeating wings.

THE SCAR ARIA

Minerva's mosquito flies only at dusk.
The bite aswell on the pale scar
left on my right ankle—a scimitar
or scythe of grainless flesh;
souvenir of a scalpeled ganglion cyst—

tells me—as I float in a net of honey locust
leaves, mulled in the word "musk,"
the word "mere," the thought of the mesh
of the shirt she wore—as much, if little more.

T.G.I.F.

While Jesus was crucified I was sitting
up in bed with Mary Magdalene, pale porcelain whore,
each already taken by the other one further time
in adultery, each of us almost dried
on the other's skin. We were watching *The Ghost*
That Never Returns by Abram Room,

marveling at the cuts. Against the slight chill in her room
(it seemed, somehow, that the sun was setting
way, way early; I'd have guessed
it was barely three in the afternoon and where
her bed lay should have been bright sun), I'd
put on a T-shirt that bragged, one further time,

"I Fucked Blair Waldorf." One further time
I had to swear it wasn't true. It was. (Her room,
a room I'd once been asked to leave, was a dread
chamber indeed, decorated with a frankly upsetting
suite of childhood photos and enough lube to make a Tijuana whore
blush. You *really* want some of that action? Be my guest.)

Anyway, the sky darkened, then this sudden gust
passed through. The earth moved one further time
that afternoon. A wire
sizzled in the wall and the now acrid room
felt as though it were starting
to fill with, I don't know, carbon monoxide.

That would have been just when he died
and everything changed, or some things did, a few, not many. His ghost
told Mary, two days after, as she was sitting
on a boulder near his once and future tomb,
"Enough with the clinging, bitch. A little breathing room,
for Christ's sake." She wore

it well, or weathered it, whatever, tough, teflon whore
that she was. Her last true tears had dried
so many years before. I was in the room
on that day, was even, you could say, the honored guest.
I remember marveling at the cuts as she took it one further time,
I remember standing in awe of the flesh she was shedding.

After that it would have been her setting out again to come never anywhere
near the longed for end, to fall down and bleed one further time. When he died
it meant nothing to me, next to, just one more ghost in the room.

OCELLE

The way that silver ring of hers—
itself joined to itself within a bored
sphere of silver—the way it loops down
through a little slipknot of flesh and hovers
over the eye of her smooth brown
belly like a molten drop grown hard

as it falls, or fell, that's the eyespot at the heart
of what's happened since she shook
her towel out and lay down, dripping wet
in her mismatched bikini, yards away,
barely, upped her knees a bit and set out
to annoy me with her body, that's the part
that pierces me—like whether it's "mistaken" or "mistook"—
that's the part that pricks me through the day.

DEBASEMENT

Long since now it's been more than I can manage —
the very sight of what I want a wrench in the system,
a tumor in the pulse that withers as it rises, weak at the base

and wavering from the get go under its own slight weight: optics, cortex, basal
ganglia — all this topline equipment and still it manages
to break down, as though it knew what I paid for the system.

Here's what it is: her Minoan head lists heavy as a sunflower on the slender stem
of her neck, itself strong as a column of basalt,
and, yes, I'm distracted by that, as you can imagine.

Here's what it is: even if I did manage
to get to second or, good Lord, third base
with her, I'd be so soon pinioned in the legal system,

to say nothing of the intense inane, that you'd see me systematically
broken down — like Cool Hand Luke, say — and this humble *menage
à deux* I'm longing for would result in my complete personal debasement

and destruction. No, it's safer to keep desire in the basement
and avoid her eyes when we meet. I can't fight the system.
What can it matter if that leaves me like a cat with the mange?
However it goes I'll just have to manage.

CHINE

I'd be thumbing the knuckles of her spine
just as soon as she'd let me in
the door. To say I'd taken a shine

to her would be like singing less than one line
of a good song. I'd lick the length of her shin
each time we'd meet—now, that's the sign

of a heart on fire, proof, if needed, of God's design
in bringing us together to suffer and sin.
He had it in for us from the starting line,

that fucker. I'm sorry to whine.
She didn't sin,
she wouldn't know how: lost, listless, supine.

She didn't sin, the sin was mine.

TRAVELER

So, do you want the Lewinsky?
MASSEUSE AT THE RUSSIAN BATHS

On the road to Eleusis
I met that girl
who bled my penis
of its string of pearls.

It was just before dark,
I was high as the Pope,
when she pushed me back
down the slippery slope.

The length of her calf
was vined with ink.
She finished me off
in the bedroom sink.

In the bedroom bath
I sank like a stone,
leaking ergot of rye
and a fifth of cologne.

RETURN JOURNEY

I've taken the narrow road to the deep north.
I've hard nosed the highway.
Now I sit in one of the dives in Firth

listening to Sid Vicious work over "My Way"
on the jukebox while a black-backed gull
wavers in a rain to end all rains

and the barmaid gives my pint another pull.
I'm wondering if she'll blow me for my pains
when the dayshift's over and she's led

me down the primrose path and up the steep
blue stairs to her low white bed.
I'm thinking I'd better watch my step.

THE HARD WAY

AFTER DANTE ALIGHIERI
Al poco giorno e al gran cerchio d'ombra ...

I've hiked up to the weak light and the wide shade,
where the hills
whiten, where the color's bled from the grass.
Still, my desire's green
as ever, so set is it in the hard stone
that talks and listens like a girl.

She's cold, this girl,
cold as snow in the shade;
she could care less than a stone
does that this sweet season warms the hills
and changes them again from white to green,
covering their sides once more with flowers and grass.

When she puts on a grass
crown, I can't even think of another girl,
because she weaves the yellow and green
so perfectly that Love sits down there in the shade —
the same Love that's shut me up among low hills
as though they were walls of stone.

She's brighter than a gemstone;
the wound she's given me won't be stanched with grass:
so I've run off over the hills

hiding from this dangerous girl;
but from her light nothing gives shade—
not hills, not walls, not summer's green.

A while ago I saw her dressed in green—
so pretty she could have made a stone
feel this love I feel even for her shade;
so, as one does with a fine girl,
I sweet-talked her, out in a field of grass
ringed with high hills.

But the streams will head back uphill
before Love's flame burns in this damp, green
wood—the way it burns in a young girl—
for my sake, who'd be a stone
lifelong, or willingly chew grass,
just to see the hem of her dress, or even its shade.

Dark as the hills give out their shade,
under her greenleaf this girl
covers it, like a stone covered in grass.

MASSAGE

The fleeting smiles, our deviating lives,
her fingers labor in my flesh —
the one expending what the other saves.

An hour into this. Another of the city's caves
of work and pleasure. Money paid to thresh
the blood. Nothing but a bed, a sheet, ourselves,

the scent of laundered breastmilk in the fan-blown scarves —
island moth and sunburst — that sash and hush
the windows' light, each one expending what the other saves.

Her hand slips slightly and a nail edge graves
my chest, a thin red line that soon enough will vanish
like her fleeting smile, our deviating lives.

I'll take the little wound. Its tattoo gives
a token of the hour and feeds the wish
to spend with one vein what another saves.

And then our silence — hers that pushes, mine that grieves —
it's just enough, for now, to nourish
these last fleeting smiles, our deviating lives,
the one expending what the other saves.

TWO-PART BELIEF

Everything will be lost, the lucid
dreams, the thimbled drams of cobalt
sunk with living dark, the unsaid

words and those we spilt
for hours on air, on fiber optic
wire, her pallid wen, the little welt

you left across my back
that gave it all away—
the welt, the welter, the long black

veil of your long black hair, the way
it wound in one soft volute
down. The welt, the words, the way

of the world we could never get right,
the wish, above all, to be just where we were.
The wen, the welter, the western light

from my opened windows as the clear
end of day hovered at a halt
there, balanced on the evening air for hours,

until we saw that dark blue felt
curtain drain down and knew with no need
to say so that it all would be lost—cell salts,

sea salt glows, seraphim and cherubim, lead
and golden echoes, lies,
the done, the doer, and the deed,

the raw and the cooked, the wed and unwed,
the weight of the world we could never surmise,
the fawn-like legs of that folding bed.

II. WE'RE ALREADY THERE

We're already there, and the day's end
stalls for good now with its patches of pale
yellow light hung between towers under

the dark. We're already there. Still,
wait, please, breathe a minute,
and let the wash of hushed time heal

the hurt girl you once were. Finite
no more, feel the stiff stuff of it slip
from your shoulders as the night

waits always now just under the lip
of that world out there—green, grown,
stone and glass, sweet mottled globe, the whole asleep.

Stand still, arms up, and be dressed in the gown
of the moment, long and lasting
for once, for once your own.

Even the rain hangs
even, a thin green wave, on which we'd waited,
even the season's blossomings,

and the seam at which we're wedded
now seals tight, with not a blister
or blemish, with not a drop bled

from its core,
not a thread of it given to rust,
to regret or despair,

and the last of it, the last whisper,
goes on that way, goes on until you can rest
here, now, where you were, where we are.

THE COARSE AIR

FOR JIM JACOBS

Such brevity, and the long slow decline
  from it, the evershining genuine impulse
lit still (how else?) but distant now, so distant
  that an instant's turn to look back towards
its little light, lamp in a wood of words and urges,
  hauls the heart up short, a halt that verges on pain
so sharp is the loss it offers, and again brings to mind—
  to the body itself, really, all of it, nerves wound through
the length to the tips and edges, blue blood coursing
  across the brain, the breast, the wrist, versing the system
(leaf, branch, and stem) in this moment's carryings on—
  and again summons, then, if that's better,
a rush of images, rushes, still, in motion, bitter, toxicant,
  deluding, silencing, of such a silence one can't do more
than stop, stunned, before them, after. In the end, of course, it all backs
  up, clotting the mind with what it's known—the facts, the lies, the dim
undone enactions, the sacrificial, grim, uplifting throbs of pleasure
  or humiliation—all this swells, dropsical, hiatal, the cincture tightens
and the weight of light which thought to brighten to preserve even something
  at least of this distends till it weighs nothing and is gone.
Before it does, before it's done, what else is there to do but take
  the moment "simply for the moment's sake" and nest within
the traces spun from all the time you've moved among before. Cup
  hands and sip from what's still falling, particles and free
complectionary flakes of air. Allow the day to gather
  or deliver—along with peregrines and double-tailed

swallowtails, *sauza añejo*, chain-winches, flash flood rubble, heat lightning,
    giardia, and road signs promising an ever greater distance yet
to go with each mile traveled—a set or suite of photograms
    on cerebellal cibachrome, a colored flood of thought that stems from long
unthought of lingerings, winding me from the pathrailing shadows in St. Stephen's Green
    sometime almost late in 1969 to the ceiling's present clean reflected shadowy
reflection: a row of balusters (wild pomegranate flowers that rail my balcony) filmed
    on the meltwater spread thin away from the stopped drain then cast
by the sun upwards and inside to rest and rustle above my head like ordinary Venetian
    light: the splay of it somehow calling to mind a girl in an ultramarine sweatsuit—
legs tucked neatly away for this my first look at her beauty, bright polish on her bare
    toenails, bright black hair,
mysteries of persistent desire, of despair even—
    who even as I write these words has or well might
have her crampons set lightly into the frozen waterfall
    at Ouray, Colorado, the tall ladderless
flume of ice she climbs like a ladder, less intent
    on the helmeted head of it, the downbent plume
at the crest, than on the momentary fume of air
    she's stencilled against just now, black hair tucked
under her stiff blue polartec cap, a just-fucked look
    softening the lines of her fine face (the book I wrote about
her so far out of her mind *maintenant* I could have written
    it on water), consummate cheekskin bitten by wind, in her mouth a coarser breath
of air than what I breathe. She's working. My mind's a slate.

A mound of earth outside the Roman gate
    at Arles; a doddering sunsmitten sunflower on a roadside near Elizabeth,
New Jersey; a bout of flies above a hidden body, copperplating its unwritten
    epitaph on the air of Hole-in-the-Rock Trail or Lookout

Mountain; and this: one stone stacked on another until the stook
     cambers in the ancient midday glare, a fresh deity licked
dry by light, a stone mushroom grown by hand and left there
     as though to show a god sprent from this desert hot as the Western Cwm
with its windless radiant fields of snow, its coruscant
     sidereal embankments: the mind that dispossesses
itself so steadily under time might stay faithful
     to, might even abide forever by so bright
and bare an image of its own solitude, its heaven
     of utter simplicity, its where-there-
is-nothingesque pursuit of mere
     being, merer becoming. Gentians, bluets,
blue ballast in the sacred plenitude of life's unrecorded passing, each incarnation
     overwhelmed in time, each delicate puzzle: what Pushkin meant by "the cast
of her eyes"; the spidery veins of one wild iris; the way the sea is calmed
     and lightened by rain until the green shadow of that scow
set upon it like a long, low temple can hardly be called green
     anymore; the chrome gleam of the ceiling
at Ménerbes, so fat was the sun on its white or cream
     crude plasterwork, and how it shed down again on her ghost pausing at the lancet
to hold the scene in mind, the brightness of the day only heightening
     that other brightness—all of this recalled
in one free moment stolen from an afternoon I'd otherwise rather
     forget. All this and more. We'd hiked to the top, the three
of us, the trail up Deer Creek Canyon through ripped
     sheets of mist, and we'd stopped for a break, coming down,
at a stone pool fed by a horsetail waterfall, no rattlesnakes
     now though earlier something moved there then was gone.
On the lip we sat and shared some gorp and croutons, then waded under the singing
     water, so pure and cool in that baked air. She had a brace of pitons

strung on her bottle belt and with one of them she scored

      our three names into the lax red mud within the rim

of a single heart—one more scrip of marginalia on the great codex,

      one insignificant hieroglyph. Before

we left there the water had begun its disintegrant

      lapping on and over who she'd said we were.

And here's whoever I am walking home through Central Park as you crest at an elevation

      of 10,666 feet crossing Vail Pass in a blizzard, strewn seed of a cloud system

rending itself in two on the western peaks, and while you're cursing

      a truck driver hard on your bumper what I've got in mind is this shore of blue

ice shelved out from the reservoir's granite edge; the stained evening air with no wind

      to it, none; the tall apartments on the verges standing in light from a moon

stalled somewhere or rising still, the towered palaces: and then the whole of it merges

      into a sort of scent—ageless, faint as death—and for once I have no words

for it, not a one, though my pulse is steady and my eyes clear, it's just that I can't

      believe it's all mine, for now, ours, all this, all this then nothing else,

not one thing else. Not one thing else. Imagine.

II

POEM BEGINNING WITH A LINE

FROM ANDREW DICE CLAY

So there I was with my tongue up her ass, half-aware even then of the misery her pleasure would bring me. The tang of asperity at the tip would have been enough to fill me in, if I had wanted to cringe with foresight at the ill-written letters of recrimination, the buses empty at midnight, the insistence of each of us on our solitary, incommunicable pain. Already at the heart of it my stomach had that sour crumpling hollow hunger I would come to know with greater intimacy at moments more torturously prolonged than this one and less intoxicated with mere sensation.

But, hey. It's not as though it would have done me much good to turn back at that point.

She had turned over, her face buried in the soft pillow of whosever bed this was and turned so that air could reach her nostrils and the side at least of her opened mouth. Not to be breathing in feathers. Before going in I had this view of her spine bowed tight like the keelstem of a trireme, each linked knuckle of it set off and softened by the stretched skin. A drop of sweat trembled at the prow of her back, ready to sluice towards the nape of her neck. Hidden in that long black hair she had her head seemed far away, her face so small with the eyes closed. An alpine breathlessness possessed me then passed on.

Rain that had fallen earlier still held to the windowpane close by the side of the tall wooden bed. Other houses and the spaces between them out there. Now the whole city was exhaling after the shower, backyard gardens, thin sidewalk trees. Light was provided through that high uncurtained window, through the wayward gaps distancing the doorframe from the door. The fluorescent bulb locked within a thick white plastic ingot above the mirror in the bathroom down the hall—I'd put it on before waking her up—fed into this in the vague impressive way light has of making more of itself than seems likely from the amounts of it spilled. But there was a lambent light on her as well, from off of her I might better say, as if I'd left it there when my tongue passed over her imperfectly.

We'd been at this for some time. Not wanting an end once we'd begun. Hunger afraid to be sated. You get to where it hardly matters whose body this is you're feasting on, so close to one another you've come. That intimacy should result in such present distance is strange but it does go that way. At one point I'd come up from between her thighs and was resting my wet lips on one of her surprisingly sharp ilia, covering her crosswise in a way I found comforting, and she'd given me this look like, Do I know you? Did she? My own thoughts were elsewhere when I saw her eyes. As with most things it's a struggle to keep the mind pinned to the present task.

That morning I wouldn't have seen it coming to this, despite the desire we'd both of us practically acknowledged, how we had talked not even uneasily around the existence of my wife, her fiancé, the way we had pretended time didn't include us. I must have been kidding myself. Baywater gathered under the restaurant dock we ate on, sun kept off the table by one of those square seaworthy heavy canvas umbrellas spread pyramidally above us on wooden ribs. An edge of it unshaded with her hand there, at ease. Icewater with its own shadow in the shadow of its glass. There are the eyes and what they do, invisibly almost. Words you've known but never said before come if they're needed, everything turned on and working, the predictable small failures falling away and forgotten as you extend it step after further step out over air that might even uphold you, hardly bothering to worry if it will. Maybe it's a game but it's difficult to see why we don't just go on playing it. What gives?

My palms to push her cheeks apart that little necessary way, thumbs plying at the almost grainless skin there, might have been parting heavy silk curtains weighted with lead. Sweat lets the fingertips slip and then take. You come to these junctures in life and you think how did I find my way here, where did I learn *this*? Mysteries of a craft hardly passed down from one artisan to the next. Nothing but darkness to wander alone in, hearing that other voice perhaps not an echo, feeling your way towards it. The back of her hip I leaned my forearm against while shifting our weight was cushioned enough to bear it without the bones aching, mine at least. But I don't want to talk about her as though she were upholstered. Had she changed, I wondered, from when I'd seen her first? With some of her I had no grounds for comparison. The cut of her face less soft, the line of the arms familiar.

She'd been visiting friends of the friends we'd been visiting in Mexico. A kind of second honeymoon for us, not long after the first. Her sister it was, married to a painter. They had a big mission house at the top of the cliff, a blue-tiled belltower, the pathway up to it rough with stones. You learn your way around places and then you never go back. That afternoon on the low leather horsehair couches in the living room there, the rug freckled with red wine from the night before, with the light tempered gray and the rain off the ocean scourging the wide windowpanes. Desultory, fierce for a moment then a patter. She had sat beside my wife and they were talking. One becoming the other. A silver clasp held her dark hair tight low near its end, the length of it hung over the one shoulder so that the far curve of her neck was bare, flesh there with a dull polish in the obscure light. Arms sunstruck bronze darkened not cooled by a cloud hung under the sun.

A few letters, more phone calls, not many. I'd seen her just one other time before this time, at a party in New York at Christmas. We were leaving as she arrived, with the coats already and nothing for it but to see her that minute and go. That long night awake. Now on the bedside table in an alabaster ashtray was a pine cone opened like a thin wooden rose. Of a shape I'd not seen before. Cedar, hemlock. Fallen on the same mountain, maybe, where this wild iris grew before it was photographed and the photograph framed and hung on the wall above the headboard. Someone had taken the little time to place it there, tapping the nail through tape into the old plaster, catching the crumbs of it in a cupped hand held to the wall like a stoup. An Indian blanket the bed had shed for us hours ago lay crumpled among a sheet on the floorboards. These weren't her things, I know—even the earrings, all she still wore, small silver rings, were borrowed—but she's taken them on, in my mind, as though she'd put them out to be thought of as her thoughts. So that they could be read as background by the light of her body. So that, after, the world itself would remind me of her.

When I'd come into town and called she'd given me a place to stay and I'd stayed there in the other room the night before, but this night I couldn't. It wasn't her place to give. After I woke her up we talked. I sat on the edge of her bed and we'd talked for a while, me trying to read her eyes, her thinking her thoughts, saying the words she said, brought to her from such distances. Strange that words remain a part of it at all, planted along the edges like reminders of some other existence. It's difficult to stop talking but you do stop.

And so I found myself feeding at her, tongue circling the rippled selvage of her body, where she ended, the outside of her, cinched tight against me at first by an invisible drawstring I loosened in time.

And so I've commemorated it. There are these words if nothing else to say that it happened. You sleep and it passes, it passes and then you sleep. But I couldn't sleep and I'd kept her up and woken her so long that the last time if it's even fair to separate them out must have been like a fever dream for her, so pliant with exhaustion she was. The way the light grew once we came towards morning made me want to stay there running my fingertips against the harp of her hardened, helplessly rising ribs. It hardly seemed ended, even as the last notes hung there, inaudible, over. I had to hold myself back as I held her sleeping and when that became too much I slipped away and out into the morning.

The sidewalk was dry except for the odd patch and then it ran out after a while and was just a road I walked up. Steep tarmac, mica caught in it beginning to glimmer. Not a car. Later they'd come for the view. The center of the road was darker than the rest of it and I noticed that, but what I thought about as I walked was the sadness of runway lights, the red lights that blink atop of water towers, the length of sunset in comparison with dawn.

At the peak was a low wooden dolmen of sorts. I sat there and looked out. Sun flensing the dark ocean, so large it seemed close from this height.

Things begin moving; maybe they'd never been still.

Down the slope a pair of young drunks were talking over the sunrise. The night before they would remember, when they'd pushed it far and then farther than the others they were with until it was just the two of them who had this morning to tell of. They would be asleep on the hillside soon, jackets between them and the grass still wet from the night's rain. Soon I'd be gone. I had to sleep myself, eventually. There would be the first words to begin its unraveling. Within a few years, after much bitterness and deception, we would have our last short conversation over the phone, on a morning when I needed no further sorrow. No, it didn't begin at once, that misery. My balls ached, true, but for the moment I still had the feel of her flesh like mercury rubbed along my veins. The way she'd pushed back against my silver tongue as though it were solid. How it had ended almost in silence, a piece of a word from her only as I worked my arm out from beneath her and she turned in sleep, letting some shadow or other pool for the meanwhile in her clavicle. Coracle. Cortés and Coronado. She would never know a thing about me. I had the whole of it to myself for now, pulsing, like I was alive in its cupped hands. But what did I know. Whatever that was it was already gone.

III

THE HUNCHBACK OF NUESTRA SEÑORA

DE REFUGIO IN MATAMUROS

She gave me water when I asked for gasoline
and a match. It was the end of my worst day.
For hours I'd been bound to this flogging machine

while some *pendejo* in a Zorro mask worked to clean
my clock with his impressive, I guess, array
of torture devices and the latest in a long line

of idiot peasants did his or her best to bean
me with a rotten tomatillo. To say
I wasn't digging this would be an almost obscene

understatement. I felt like I was bleeding Valvoline.
The sanctuary of the cathedral was only yards away
but I had as good a chance of reaching Abilene

or Amarillo. The whole sick thing had been
staged as a kind of sadistic holiday:
speakers blared Santana's "Black Magic Woman/Gypsy Queen,"

old men drank mezcal from the bottle, and gangs of pre-teen
temptresses danced like Jezebel. Then this grey-
eyed beauty, out of nowhere, brought me water, cold and clean.

Love binds you to the source of your pain,
feeds you what you hadn't craved before, then takes it away.
She gave me water when I asked for gasoline
and still I'm bound to the flogging machine.

GHOST

If it wasn't the long
Sucked-in bellows of a plane passing
Overhead
While this rain makes like the wind
As far as direction goes and speed, I'd
Swear it was her ghost again working to stop my heart.

Not that I don't find it hard
To stay shivering for very long
Even though I'd
Rather be set atremble by the faintest passing
Shade or sound than let the wind
Blow empty rain against my fearless head

While I go on hardly taking heed
Of what's happened to my heart,
To call it that, since she's been gone. Unwind
Is what they all tell me, when they bother, but the long
And short of it is that she wasn't a passing
Flame or fancy and if I'd

Thought to be free of her this soon, or ever, then I had
Something wrong with my head.
If that wasn't passion
Then this isn't my heart
Throbbing again now after that long
Full stop when she touched my nape like a piece of wind

Out on a spree. Admittedly, I'd like to rewind
The tape to the ides
Of February, the 13th not the 15th, that one night so long
Ago now I must be old. Head
I gave her. Heart.
As I held her I could feel it all passing.

Home, out of the rain, I'll sip my poison
And listen to the wind
Blow hard
Against my life. Having eyed
Her I can't get her out of my head.
She'll be with me while I am, however long.

I'm wrong. Nothing but a plane passing overhead
And a wind I'd be hard
Pressed to tell it from if it, the wind, didn't last nightlong.

TRYST

Still, while the workfare slaves rake leaves
And trash in the slow, fog-sunk morning
We'll make the little effort needed to forget
Their sufferings below and rest what grieves
In our own lives aside and tie the knot
Again the hour will see untied, still learning

The ropes of one another's veins, the nerves
To stroke or tug to some involved release
Of tenderness or pain, those discomposing
Tremors won from trembled flesh that strives
To rise against the air it's cased in, losing
Sense of sense, of touch, of breath, of ease.

We'll be slow to rise and take the time
To come apart and find our thoughts gone far
Off, susurrous and soft as clouds. Who cares?
The wet cuffs of the tired and tiresome
Men at work will harden when the air
Around them dries, they'll die, and our own scars

Will bear so little weight beside those lives
Of pain and want we'll want to hide above
The come-and-go and let the pleasure last
A minute more, an hour. If time forgives
This waste of time we're saved, there's nothing lost,
Nothing wrong with life lived at one remove.

Knowing nothing's kept for long we'll hold
Awhile to what we have before it's swept
Away—the windowlight; the sound of leaves
Raked over the cold concrete; the bald
Lies we'll soon forget we told; the lives,
Unlived, of those who suffered as we slept—

And praise the day that brought us here to sin,
To find the pulse of what we feel and see
And let the rest roll on as though we rested
On the nape of a wave gone past, smooth as linen
Fresh from the iron's press: still, untested,
Sunblind, finished, floating, silent, free.

PARCHMENT

I don't write and the night stays put,
Dead to her dear forgotten face.
The darkwood furniture gives the place
Its air of death, as from a window shut
Against the sun it can't keep
    Out. I can't sleep.

The air holds nothing but I breathe it still.
A clutch of tallstemmed flowers draw
Last draughts of life through the green straws
Of their own cut throats. I'm ill
With confusion. She's hardly real
    Anymore. I feel

A weight that's neither hers nor mine
Heavy in the muscles of my chest and legs and back,
Solid in the airless bag of my stomach,
Pressed along my spine.
She's casketed inside me like a reef of shit.
    I'm blind to it

But not entirely unawares. Now let me say
A word about her beauty. It was of the kind
That answers with such lit grace the mind
That summons it that to stay
Far from her kind long as I've now done
    Is to be gone

Out like a light, out from life
As it seems worth going on with. Explain?
How, when eyes close and she's gone
And nothing of her to live on? A leaf
Falls with equal loss and beauty. She's
     One of these

Girls we all long to look at longer
Than the others. As lovers
They never bear up; the heart withers
Before the eyes grow tired; they're younger
Always than the mind has time for. It's nights
     When the lights

Burn till morning, after, and the eyes rasp
Against the lids, that's their reign.
Like this night. Throat dry tinder. A cold rain
Falling would relieve this air beyond the grasp
Of my old lungs. I miss her.
     Whoever kissed her

Lids when we last parted
Must have known her from another
Beauty. Now I can hardly bother
To conjure the color of her eyes. See, it's started:
Desire born fresh from its own ashes, fire
     Kindled to expire.

THE DISAPPOINTMENT

And who should I say I love if not
you? Seana Ryan? Winona Ryder?
That blonde girl a decade back on the LIRR,
her eyelashes mirrored
on the sunlit window as the train
we rode edged out from under the white- and red-

painted iron trelliswork of Long
Beach station some uneventful summer morning?
The list could go on:
the names, the half-remembered faces,
barrow after barrowful of limbs and torsos gathered from within the radius,
as it were, of the shell by which they were blown

apart, scraps of flesh lodged in a mind unable to rid
itself of a never quite blossoming and yet not
to be shaken or dislodged habit of desire, the strain
of which shivers through me still, as a rider
feels along his spine the ground the hooves beat hard,
as fingertips sting from the strings of, yes, the lyre

they keep plucking at with small success, one blown
melody after the next, the long
hours spent for nothing but that sting. Our Chevy Malibu's A.M. radio,
do you remember, offered up Dylan's "New Morning"
as we crossed the Blue Ridge by the western road that faces
Shenandoah Mountain, halted at the crossroads, then turned north on

Route 11. The glare
of sun on the windshield, the blacktop, the bright red
leaves of sugar maples—that hard querying light mirrored
or bodied forth the sense we shared of simply not
knowing. Riderless horse or horseless rider—
it was all the same to us, more or less. We did know this—that rain

would fall on
other lives, if not our own, that blown
leaves would settle over this stranger's grave, tears line the faces
of his sisters (our friends then), of his father and mother, his life, the long
spun gathering of what he was, cut off just the morning
before by a drunken salesman asleep at the wheel, radials

tending unreined over the parallel yellow lines. A train
passed in the distance as the box of him went down to its private cellar.
I already would be, this I knew, a writer.
(Somewhere, I'm certain, I still have the brownish-red
notebook of that time, though I cannot
or will not look at it now, mired

as I know it must be, given the general raininess
of late adolescent agons
and maunderings,
in wholesale self-engorgement, emotions blown
out of all just proportion, the desire to belong,
if only to oneself, a craving not even time effaces.)

I look back at that moment, those moments, as at a mirror
in which only the traces of images, a sort of bridal train
trailed by vanished presences but not
the presences themselves, hover under a glaze or glair,
uncertainly, gleam there. If I could have read
the years to come, the brighter

hours, the dark and bitter, in the faces
gathered by that new grave, hers, yours, each life set on its own bent radius,
would I have longed
for us to go on
otherwise, or thought to weigh the loan
of our brief destined pleasures against their attendant mourning?

What would you rather?
The stuck fate of a life mirrored
back upon its own fixed and fading image, red
blood going to brown as the life drains
from us, less like Lear
with his *aria virile*, his daughter dead in his arms, than Babo picking at that knot

of oakum, plotting against the aged morning?
What else can I set against this death but the names, the passing faces
taken at a glance, the eyes met and remembered, the blown
chances and the chances taken: to be moving, to extend the radius
just an inch or so of my known world, of ours, to go on
a piece with what we won't be going on with long?

This is me. Alone in the dark I read by these: the gold-red hair of Venus, the train
of wavelets the morning gives to carry her along;
the sunken spine of Sasha Grey; bold Victorine Meurend; the daughters of Lir
with their swan faces bent upon
the water they ride, awaiting change; your face; hers—their light not
less than I need, the light from a blown fuse, light enough, light or some other radiance.

WHAT HER SISTER TOLD ME

I'd never thought of her, I suppose,
as human, so that the news
that she'd been ill, mysteriously —
her stomach cankered (nothing like a rose),
fisted by some plague that had seriously
fucked her spring and winter — was like a dose

of some bad thing for me as well,
a bright cramp that would double
its silent decibel of pain as it spread
through the moist naïve unmuscled
organs piled between my ribbed
upper torso and my lonely cock and balls.

It had been a long time now since
she'd speak to me or take my calls, hence
the immense dilation of her sexy
evanescent presence in my mind, hence
my surprise at what her sister told me,
the shock I had from it, its slow subsidence.

She had been living in Baltimore,
she said, a nursing student at Hopkins (where
my novel had languished long on the desk
of John T. Irwin; where years ago my mother
had shepherded my anorexic bro' to ask
the counsel of yet another big time witch doctor),

and this thing had just come on, her desire
to eat shaved down at last to the point where
she wouldn't anymore from the pain
it caused her, her admittedly never-
too-fucking-stable mind perched again
on the brink of a long-hedged disorder

known to her by her father's years of shock
therapy, known to us all by the slack
uncurrented dark upwelling ambient
sadness that laps at the back
of most lives and lets the mind undo the lent
body with a tap, a tap, a long persistent suck.

In that novel of mine her body had been given
under the face and temper of a friend of my cousin—
a brighteyed babbling girl from Miami, Ohio:
all that remains of it there is a colorless wen
high on the downslope of her pinioned torso
"where her last left rib last tents the skin";

all that remains of the night that I fit
my mouth to her crotch and went at it
hammer and tongs is an iodonic salty tang,
a vague recollection of the feel of her clit,
its slight weight resting on the tip of my tongue,
the wish to retaste it, the knowing I'll not.

That that charmed flesh should ever fail or fall
was a prospect which had evaded my dull
mind through all its fevered glancings back
to the soft borrowed bed where she lay in blissful
(I'd like to think) disarray, her long black
hair, blue in its undertones as the shell of a mussel,

astray on the white pillowcase, the cambered
gleam of her grainless limbs now turned
in fetal disavowal of the sweated hours
we'd just come through intact, entwined,
when what was hers seemed mine and mine ours
and its certain impermanence had not yet registered.

I don't think quite so often of our final conversation
in which I hardly spoke a word. Her recitation
of a venomous letter she'd just opened
from my wife (not quite long-suffering as per convention)—
"fucked my husband" & "your former friend"
are two phrases I recall—was our terminal punctuation.

*

Never to be fed, what once was called the heart—
glob of come-clotted muscle breaded in the mind's dirt;
mold-rotted still-life plum on which a housefly stirs—
hungers, yearns, its sound like the fiddle at the start
of *Serenade* that weeps its hard dry tears
for the body's unmet wants, its loss of comfort,

its sad unconsummating daily stand in "the desolate
market where none come to buy"; the late
evening clouds over Cedar Hill, where I lie
on my back in the cut midsummer grass, a celibate
hedonist adrift in the real world of the mind's eye,
have gone from apricot to a bright hulled pomegranate

wet against the deepening sky (a color in which I can't
help but see the splayed liquid membrane of her cunt,
hers or some other's—all wanted things
in the end tending to get lost or leveled in the rampant
course of lust's imperatives and burgeonings,
its childish refusal to be still or silent);

where she is now and what it is that grows
within her, or has died, there'd be no purpose
in my trying to discover. No, she's rid of me.
what will be the long result of what she chose
and what I chose we'll have to wait to see
but never see and then forget then recollect then lose

the thread of after all. This is the way a life fills
and what it fills with: raw deals,
sour grapes, death and pleasure,
the live and random care for how another feels,
the tandem disregard, the treasured body's ruined structure.
I hope she's healed. I hope she heals.

IV

AISLING

In the groundmist above the mown grass, under the bronze maple, out beside the swimming pool, I saw her in that rich blue light that fills the air just before sunrise, a tube of tanning oil in her hand and a beach towel hung over her arm, tortoiseshell sunglasses pushed back like a hairband over her wet blonde hair, her breasts heavy against her white halter top, flat stomach the color of polished butternut, long spaghetti ties in a single loose knot at each flared hip, fine muscled legs, bare feet, toenails painted red and wet by the morning dew spun over the lawn she would spread the towel on soon enough, to lie out and let her flesh accept the sun's rays later when they came.

I stopped her as she crossed the flagstone path by where the slate steps lead down to the tennis court gate and I stood there a moment without speaking, so taken was I, stunned really, by her beauty, the weight of it I might say, and by the way it brought back to me the memory of a girl I'd watched once at this same blue hour, decades ago now, from the window of a little spare bedroom with pale red curtains in the guest house of some family friends, where my brothers and I had slept after a summer party, and of how that girl, lovely then, older than us, a teenager, in tennis whites, racket in hand, had come to such grief over the years and brought such pain to herself and those who loved her, the ones who'd made her body from their own.

What had brought her there so early, I asked, before the full sun was ready to be on her, darkening her tan, soothing even the depths of her muscles with its heat? And she told me she had come to answer the questions she knew I had for her, if I could ask them. I had gone out to the yard myself as though drawn there, a sleepwalker under the sway of an unseen hand, and the thought that I had come to seek answers dawned only as she said so, though I'd sought my first already. This was my task, it seemed, and the work waited, but my breath held a moment as I took her in, hesitant to inch the day on with the next word.

Cloudberry flowers laced the low green plantings at the edges and there was a lighter green veining her pale blue eyes, where I saw no reflection of myself but only her own lashes enmeshed there with the underbranches of the bronze maple and the bent blue distance glazed between. We stood in the yard that joined her house to mine like a ligament—a strange piece of shared earth unlike any other in the town —and I asked her in what way I'd be paid for holding still so long, in wait for it all to begin, and would there never be a day that held still in turn, was there no rest ahead from time that moved away always beneath us, beneath the grass, beneath the ground, erasing us, and I told her of the grief I felt beforehand at how things would go for her, the certainty with which I knew that her beauty, strong as it was, could never be redeemed here, and if not here then nowhere.

In the kind, pitying look she gave me, her expression held in a sort of porcelain calm as when a young mother watches her child fall down again to the warm sand he struggles to walk on, I saw for a moment, in a sudden revelation, the likeness of that woman whose blue eyes had harbored my own, and I asked of her too, would I see her again, here or hereafter, knowing I wouldn't, knowing I never would. A swallow dipped to sip from the pool without breaking flight. From a neighbor's window a radio played Whitesnake's "Here I Go Again On My Own," loud for the hour and soon extinguished but a sign that the world made its way on without us, as always, and she told me that no rest waited ahead and that things would never be made right, the tear in the cloth would never be sewn.

In the long silence that followed her words she showed me the golden rooms, or gray, where love banks its dying flame, the great crowded beaches where nameless others burned away the measured fuses of their lives under the hot sun, an empty yard glazed with pitted ice, a cold slope of grass under the moonlight, the first tussle in the dunes and the last walk home at night, and I thanked her in that by the power of her blossoming there she blent this all for us into one heavy drop, and in that she gave her blessing to our driven blood, caught in its own round even as we felt it drying, and I knew from her that we'd never be more easily set in place than at this moment we shared just then.

Unaware that I had, I'd gone down to my knees and I reached out to run my fingertip along that little rift of untanned skin at the verge of her thigh but just as I touched the soft flesh there she vanished and I was left stroking the trembling air. She moved away soon after that and I heard that her marriage had taken a bad turn and then that her family had split apart, the blonde children shuttled between states and the whole weight of life heavy on what idea of her I was ever able to call to mind, but for that moment there was rest and the dead spoke to me through the mere fact of her body, the grass just starting to warm and the moon still so bright in the morning sky you could see those tiny footprints in its silver dust.

THE OUTER LIFE

AFTER HUGO VON HOFMANNSTHAL

And children grow up with deep eyes
and they know nothing, grow up and die,
and everyone goes their own way.

And the bitter fruits sweeten
and fall down at night like dead birds
and lie there till they're rotten.

And the wind blows always, and time and again
we hear words, say them,
and feel our bodies' pleasure and exhaustion.

And streets run over the grass, and here
and there are places set with streetlamps,
ponds, trees—some decrepit, some sinister . . .

What are they here for, not one
of them like another, and without number?
Why do we laugh, cry, and go white in turn?

What good is all this to *us*, all these games,
who, after all, are great, and forever lonely,
and who wander without aim?

What good is it to have seen all this?
But still, just to say "dusk" is to say a lot,
a word that bleeds profundity and sadness

like honey heavy from a hollowed comb.

ONCE WE'RE HERE

Somehow, my friend, the unhitched flatbed
car we're sitting on, tailorwise, outside
of Charlottesville, Virginia—talking
for the first time, really, while the afternoon sun

beats the dead rails of the siding
a brighter silver between the weeds and gravel—
has gotten going and has passed
along through the aquarium light of the Carlow East,

through the redwood forests of King's Canyon,
along the Zattere, under the flocked
and unflocked branches of the crabapple
tree at the heart of the tainted

garden, until we're in a tunnel of sorts, booklined
and hung with pictures of ourselves, with no sound
between us but some childish breath, a cancer's dropclock,
and the steampipe's hypnotic unwearying complaint.

THE TERRORISTS

You'd almost throttle the child for the night of sleep
he's cost you, but that aside, out before the sun,
it's good to be here with him on the scrofulous bench
while the hosts, the rest of yours, sleep on
inside—and now the sun unsilvers the morning grass,
the small birds flash and flutter their coded wings
against the light as they work the feeders, a cow
pisses hot splashes against the electric fence,
the leaves light and leaven—and lift him then
to walk the late garden and eat the last
raspberries off the spent canes, raise the gatelatch,
and climb to watch a brace of ducks trace
the undosed waters of the local reservoir
with vectral script, the words of this aubade.

THE SLEEPING LIFEGUARD

I'd only slept an hour or more
When I woke up to see the ocean wild
With waves and shot with silver
Stormlight and the children who'd been
Swimming gone under or gone.

Sand grains set in the longboard's wax
Shimmered and the sand around it shone.
Soon enough there'd be a trooper wanting facts,
Just facts. Not last night's fun. I'd seen
That girl I'd say. I had. That child.

OONA O'NEILL, 2010

That was the year I never
saw, or even thought to see, my father.
That was the year the gems I wore
were stolen while I was watching *Jersey Shore*,
along with my iPod, camera, and a $400 pair of shoes.
That was the year he paid his dues.
Even now I long to watch him write that check
time and again, sign it, watch him empty the book,
the pen, so many checks does he have to write,
as even now I might head out again into a night
ensigned with city lights, mine, and leave him written out.
That was the year I lost my doubt,
if only for that little while. The pillowcase
that took my tears, that emerald dress
I almost tripped on, running up those stairs,
are thread by thread undone these many missing years.

II.

The remains of the daydream stain me still.
Zebra-striped dragonflies low over Cedar Hill
on a sun-candoured, stunned late summer afternoon
just where he'd lain with her that one spring night, under the moon—
that girl I'll never love, but whom he loved—

then drove us down to the beach house, gone,
my head on his shoulder, goodnight moon,
all of us thinking we each would never leave.
We left.
I know he carries that weight, the heft
of my heavy little-girl's head, the warm
wash of my sleeping, inkblack hair.
That moon he misbegot us under turns
its black face away from the moonlit room
in which he sits, and writes, and never learns.
It's all I can do to leave him there.

APRÈS LE DELUGE, MOI

When the ceiling began to come down on the heads of the poets
it was still far too early for most of them
and the audience hardly knew whether to weep
or applaud at the windfall of eminent seats now to be empty.
It's difficult to say for certain if I was the first to see
the flakes of paint and plaster falling white in the stagelights
towards the wise white head of the oldest and best of them,
seated stage left after having given what was turning out to be
his last reading.

       It had been planned as a celebration
of the living word and we, its devotees, had gathered
from the far ends of the city and further out—
one friend drove down from distant Vermont in the heavy winds—
leaving our own garrets and café posts to suffer without us
a few hours while we watched (or is it listened to?—
I've never known, the right words, as always, a task to arrive at)
those who had scaled the heavens on ladders of glass
reveal themselves as ordinary men, hard to be fond of,
burdened with better hangovers than our own
and with the accumulated confusion of decades
spent doing what they'd wanted to and not working,
charming the muse into paying for drinks each night
and succouring the long morning's uncertainty and despair.

In the heady weeks that followed the formative calamity,
change was so commonly abroad in the land,

passed on the very breezes haunting the banner-hung rostrums
in the squares and sunswept fields, that it seemed each dawn
arrived in a different world. Monuments to the mighty dead
were ruins in the space of days. We walked among the broken
columns in the elation of careless gratified desire. Birds we'd never known
the names of sang in the familiar unbeloved trees to us.

So much has happened. We grow old
and the roof above our own symposium
might look unsteady if we bothered to glance upwards.

Still, I cannot believe the radiance of that night will dim.
We were all of us in a state of metamorphosis.
More than a few of those down in the front rows
turned into the predictable butterfly and fluttered
upwards out through the opened rafters and away.
A bearded man beside me, bald, was glowing like the stranger
from *The King of the Golden River*; an otter wandered
the broad red velvet handrail of the upper loge.
Most of my own friends I never recognized again,
though likely as not I met them on occasion.
I was a pill-bug the stone had been lifted from off of,
hurrying somewhere under the revealed night sun.

A PICTURE OF LITTLE C.C.

IN A PROSPECT OF FLOWERS

When my body first started changing it felt like a science project.
CINDY CRAWFORD

A technicolor starling adroit in the dry needles
pinces a honeysuckle seed in its bright beak,
pivots its head—slick crownfeathers, eyes dazzled carbuncles—
and steps away from where the vines rise thin to bind the dying pine;
a pair of Karner blues flutter unwarily above the line
between the pale flare of their own moment and afterwards; a loggerhead shrike,
looking half-undone already in its thin black mask,
impales a salt marsh harvest mouse on a long thorn then sings, as if to ask

what separates a songbird from a bird of prey;
on a bed of broomrape, fleshy owl's clover, island bedstraw
and velvet fingergrass an ocelot—froth-lipped, gold-eyed—gives up the day;
and here where perspective leads, perched on the burnished shell
of a green sea turtle, is a pregnant starlet, her bare belly
oiled for the floodlights, her fine-bred
neck laden with all she wears—a garland of autumn buttercups,
zebra mussels, yellow-shouldered blackbird and black-capped

vireo feathers, California jewelflower buds, a xenops' seed-sized brain
dried to a pod of powder, wireweed, dwarf
bear-poppies, lacy elimia shells, Red Hills vervain,
the ground wingscales of a dozen Uncompahgre fritillaries, a goldline

darter's skeleton, wire-bound sprigs of toad-flax cress, slender-horned spine-
flowers, heartleaf,
island rush-roses, Roan Mountain bluets, the interlinked
tails of a quetzal and a jaguarundi, a Kern primrose sphinx

moth that's pinned spreadwinged above her distended navel,
and at the nadir of it all a sheaf of Lane Mountain milk-
vetch from which hangs pendant a spleaf of 'O'o plumes and fractal milfoil
saucers with a yellow-toothed nutria skull dreaming hollow-eyed agape
atop her *mons veneris*. I'm practically asleep
myself in this dead air. Not even the skulk
of a guard to break the silence. The last diorama. My breath
on the glass fading to a fine sweat

as somewhere on a broad granite
beach or breast or bank of snow—
it's all the same to her—a wide breach of light
breaks in stunned continuum on the uncrystalline
skin or sand or stone, the air replete with sirens
and false goldenrod, the flow
and ply of rising tides
a flooded grave, a mirror for the clouds.

V

THE DRUG OF CHOICE

I'm waiting, while the preferable girls blade by
      tranced in a kind of grounded flight
With their legs asweep like a grass skirt swaying
      and some others walking home in heels
Give the mind an item to dream on a moment,
      if only a curl of hair lifted
From its own liquid motion by what breeze there is.
      Thanks, I'll take it. And anything else?
The sun begins its initial descent somewhere over distant Newark Airport,
      one hot star burning to expend the others
Coming out like children now to peer down from the sky's stairhead
      and I'm waiting to turn
My back on it all and ride off eastward in my brother's red Porsche
      with the top down and the looks
Of deference and envy from our fellow motorists who mean no ill
      but would be pleased to see us waiting on the side
Of the road while the trooper assiduously copies down the plates
      before approaching with his ticket and his lecture.
All right, they do mean ill, we all do, often. Their loss has made me
      laugh in turn enough times not to lie about it further.
Be that as it may, the trees in Central Park are halted in a fever of dusty summer
      growth and I'm waiting on a townhouse stoop
Across the street from them where the limestone foliage of its sandblasted
      balustrades glows in the late light and begins to release
The day's warmth basking in its pores. Sweet evening. So hot at noon, so hard not
      to talk about the weather when it is, after all, the air
We breathe, the light we have our visions by, like this one walking
      past me made of everything I'm made to want

As long as I can hold her in my sight, and after, even, as the memory
      lessens, leaving a frame or two to come
Upon, years later, against closed eyelids, on the altar of another's body.
      Or: She's pretty and I'm happy to watch her go by,
Thinking what I might have thought of to win a smile from her,
      if nothing more, "Could you direct me to wherever
It is you're headed? I seem to have lost my way." Like that, but more so,
      or less so, rather, better than—and then why bother, you think,
When there'll soon be another and to choose her now will leave the next ungathered.
      To choose: I wish. I could be walking home through the park
Upstream against the current of runners who call to mind the damned in Dante's hell
      at their ceaseless circling tasks and lead me
To wonder why I'm not burning along with them. Each comes panting
      towards me and sometimes our eyes catch a second
And maybe I'm whistling as a token of mental vacuity and then they're gone.
      There's so much desire, so little space to rest it on.
My cousin, an amiable moron, told me earlier on the telephone about a girl
      he'd met last night at a bar who grabbed his crotch
("The package," as he called it) not long after she said hello, then took him home.
      Like that. I asked what she was like and he said her entire
Vocabulary consisted of the words "dick" and "cock." You laugh, or I did,
      but acknowledge still it's all we'd need to have her know.
Girls I'd like to lick and then be loved by later leaving aside the loss of and the left-
      handed compliments, the let down, lustlessness, and l'ennui:
They pass by engaged in their own civilized lives and dreams and I'm still
      waiting for my brother in his ostentatious car to take me
Up Third through Spanish Harlem and the lower depths of Harlem where life
      rages on in all its harmful disarray and the lifers' wives
Linger in traffic to talk to one another with what words they know;
      where there's a store called Italy that's gone

Out of business and the low skyline of water tanks and dirty brick and brownstone
      holds the look that I remember of the city I grew up in,
This one, gone, though I'd rather have it back than all the cheap money
      it's washed in now. Familiar light does still wash the river
Buildings and the ugly blue bridge and the cars in fast traffic on the FDR
      and what the water adds to it rings like a tuning fork
In all the senses except touch. Yes, you can taste it as you pass, believe me, I know.
      And whatever became of Mike McNeill who tried
To taste and touch it in his tuxedo at dawn the night of the Regis prom?
      Over the railing he went, behind Gracie Mansion,
With a can of beer in his hand and a few of us caught him by the ankles
      and hauled him laughing hysterically out of the air.
A difficult friend I suppose I don't really miss. The weight of him and him
      so scrawny! Some do drown. He would have been one.
From the bridge you can see the sight of those high jinks. I like how
      the city gets scarred by what you do on it,
Anonymous scratches scratched over the already scratched surfaces
      telling nothing to nobody but a sign that something
Happened once. It's happening still. You just get tired of street life
      and long to move through it and past it.
I used to want so badly to be poor and tough and black so that my heart
      went weakly out each time we'd start
This same drive I'm waiting to make once more today, thinking myself
      not real at all beside the hard squalor of the world
On view there. No more. Today I'd rather live the good life as I can
      and rest content in the knowledge that what we want
To become hangs always out of reach, in change itself, just as the hunger to possess
      an image registers the failure to possess its object.
Here there's a red-tailed hawk atop a capital of one of the museum's giant columns
      and a pair of low lifes, anomalous on this wealthy

Block, or not, go past and one of them's saying, "You know what I'm saying—
       my girls want any more drugs they going to pay for them."
Word. I'm with you. No, I'm never sad now not to be one of them or to leave
       the city or come back to it either. I'm ready, I'm easy.
It can take so long to hit your rhythm when you're crucified with longing
       for love and sex and life and recognition and what
You know catches in the throat and sets you off balance and can't be said right
       and burns in you still long after, never allowing you to
Forget it. There's a week or so in spring when the wind strips the elm trees
       of their seeds and scatters them along the avenue
Like paper coins and they whirl about the gutters when the buses pass over
       and rise and drop in the air up outside my office
Windows and then twist in a skein when a gust comes to tear them downtown.
       I love to watch them, to see "the whole nature of the wind
As it blew that day," which is how Roger Ascham puts it in his passage on snow,
       a piece of writing I sought out and copied down in pencil
One sunny afternoon this April—the coolest month, with all things wigging out
       and blazing into change. I was at the library
No more than an hour and while I was inside the pear tree on the sidewalk
       blossomed. So much is set in motion and here we are
Midsummer and rolling with it still. Once you get through Queens, the borough
       of houses, and deep in it too, by Flushing and Douglaston,
The trees grow tall and the low stone bridges keep the trucks off the parkways
       and the sea light starts to reach you over the flat
Land, so flat that from that one elevation hard by Creedmoor Mental Hospital
       you can see the metal water towers of eleven towns
Plopped up from the horizon like a palmful of pale blue chanterelles.
       I always figured I would wind up in the bughouse
Myself, if not in prison, which should give you some idea of the taste I had
       during my exceedingly prolonged adolescence

For lachrymose passive/aggressive self-aggrandizing ruminations.

"Even here, sounding wild, he had grounds, perhaps"—

My helpful friend Ed Conlon once unhelpfully inscribed that sentence in a book

he gave me, the sentence taken from the book itself

To show he'd read it first or at least had opened it at random. And maybe I did

have grounds. It's true that my once closest friend,

Who also had a prison fixation and used to tell stories about the time

he'd done on the Rock or Rikers, managed to spend

More than a couple of years in the bin playing joyless and peculiar

mind games with the doctors and nurses

Instead of sucking tit or smoking pot or learning Greek or following the Dead

or any of the other pastimes favored by his peers.

And what's more I won't deny that I once saved the life of a guy who went on

to become a murderer. His name was Alan Blunton, is still

I imagine, and if he's become a reader of poetry since his release from Sing Sing

I suppose I should think twice before telling this story

Though I've gone so far along the path of reckless offense that I might as well fire

all of my guns at once and explode into space.

If I was twelve, which is probably right, then Alan was fourteen

or fifteen that summer which would bring us back

To 1978, down at the South Shore. Scion of a white trash bay rat family, he was hard

as iron and widely feared and admired

As the toughest thing going in town. It's pushing it but you could say we were friends.

That was the year he had stolen the gorgeous girlfriend

Of a cocky seasonal prepster named Jimmy Edsel and she was the one we heard

screaming that night, she was the one we ran along the sand to help.

What she was called I don't recollect, it ended with a *y* and it might have been Kerry,

she was a kind of mother's helper from Arizona

In the house of Frank and Tracy Doyle. One afternoon my best friend James and

Frank and I tried to spy on her in the bathroom shower

Through the backyard window and bold James reached into the steam and pulled aside
the curtain and she screamed. Her name is gone but I recall her
Wrapped in a big white towel with oxblood braiding to rhyme with her reddish
brown mane shrieking, "Did you see my body?"
As though we could have robbed her of it with our eyes. I'd seen nothing.
James claimed a nipple. It was not long after that
That he and I heard her screams along the beach. She tended to scream—an ordinary
self-enraptured heartthrob caught up in the drama of being desired.
They'd been sharing a romantic six pack of Michelob on the jetty and even though
there were still two left unopened in the holder
Alan was wasted and had started to get sick and then had pitched off the rocks
into the rising tide. We hadn't known him
As a lightweight and so concluded that he'd spiked the evening with some quaaludes.
He was vomiting face down in the flat dark wavelets
Drowning already and choking on his puke, dead for certain if the two of us hadn't slid
down the wet rocks and gotten him by the armpits and pulled him up.
In the shower at the top of the beach he stood like a punchdrunk fighter with the froth
at his mouth and his asswhipped body shivering. We had his shirt off.
Look and you'll see the flat unbulging muscles of his upper arms, the cords of his forearms
tight even in his helpless inattention to them.
I gave him my own shirt and went home that night without one. I saw him with it on
a few nights later but he never gave it back.
It was a short-sleeved navy blue sweatshirt embossed with the heraldic crest
of the New York Rangers, with
Ribbed cuffs to tighten on the biceps and if I had it back I'd wear it if it fit.
Two years later he robbed my family's summer house
With his dirtbag brother Bobby, dead now, and some other local skells.
After that we didn't hang out much anymore.
I heard he'd knocked the shit out of a little kid and tried to gouge his eyes
out with his thumb. The night he killed

A semi-retarded cabdriver on the road from Long Beach may have been
        his eighteenth birthday, I remember something
About that, how he was set to enter the Marines the morning after.
        His story was the guy had made a pass at him.
He pulled the poor dimwit out of the cab and beat him to the ground then caved
        his head in with a cinder block. After this, unsatisfied,
He drove the car back and forth over the man's body twenty or thirty times
        then left it there. He robbed him too, of course,
But where he ditched the vehicle and where he was when he was caught
        the next day I can't say. I never read a word about the murder
And haven't heard in quite some time the story told by those who know it better.
        When he arrives I'll have to remind my little brother
About that chestnut from the good old days and tell him further that his
        car is ridiculous and that we should have a suitcase
Full of cash to release from its open trunk as we burn along the highway
        except the motor's in back like a Volkswagen
And we could never drive as fast as we'll be going with the hood open.
        You forget the sufferings of others, even your own.
There's a stretch of parkway just before the town that curves across a scattering
        of marsh islands high with dunes and opens up a view
To sea at one turn and another. It's painted dangerous now with a weave
        of yellow safety lines but there once had been
A phantom lane that dwindled as the road approached the final bridge before
        the shore and there we used to die
With some degree of regularity, a mile away from done with the long drive home.
        So many went there — my father's sister
A decade younger than I am now; both parents of these handsome kids I knew;
        a highway patrolman who stopped to help
And was himself run down — I think about them all whenever I go by, a thought
        without much worth or substance.

91

What the dead want from us, who can do nothing for them except lose sight
       of the little we ever knew of their thoughts and lives:
This is a question not to be answered while the sweet light strikes our eyes
       still and we hurry after them along the same way.
I can't wait to swim tonight and if we're off soon we'll be there by last light,
       time enough to see the purple sky
Stained at the hem with other colors and mirrored on the surface of the water,
       the ocean at its endless carbonated arterial collapse.
A black lab runs far along the tideline and leaps to catch a thrown stick spinning
       through the air; swimmers emerge astream with sea water,
Figures glowing like they're after being plucked from molten glass
       and are not yet awakened to the pain they're in.
In the yard we'll sit and listen to the cicada's brief continuous telegraphic rattle
       and watch the bees working over
The tapestry wall of sweet pea, nightshade, clematis, and morning glory
       hung above a few rose bushes, yellow and white, which bloom
Fine but soon wither, the petals like wet crêpe paper clotted on the stamen.
       It all grows sweet sometimes and the love
You've wasted grows strong again if you're able to wait and let it grow.
       Now it would be good to recline in the warm arms
Of the life made for me, mostly, by me as well, in part, at times, but mine
       regardless; now it would be good to regard
The life I've led in light of the longed-for life, and look kindly on the lies
       and truths alike, letting them lie together
On the bed I've made for them, soft enough and not so bad. Time and again
       the mind turns back to moments
When the choice made was to watch what there is and say nothing and do nothing
       but soak it in and be changed.
A hasp of rope left over from the clothesline, a crab apple sprung of its flowers—
       these will be seen in the particular heavy light and mean nothing—

The wasp gone down between the slats of the steps, the tomato plants in need of tying.
     Burdock and jimsonweed, goldenrod and thistle,
They'll be living wild along the roadside up among the dying pines
     draped with vines of ivy and someone
Somewhere knows the score on why they're there and how the pappus spreads
     the seeds into the winds and lets them
Flourish without care. Not me. I barely know their names and colors
     and never will be more than ignorant.
And here I am trying to squeeze some juice from the words I've spent my lifetime
     learning. Far too few of them. Reading *Madoc* last winter
I copied out 147 I didn't know and then settled in with the big two leather
     volumes of Johnson's Dictionary to look them up and write
Out the meanings and forget them afresh. One was "grume" and another "rumen."
     It can be hard to know the weight
To give to things, how many hours to spend on useless words bereft and adrift
     in the wastes of this dead language,
The only one I have. On any given day I cannot say with any certainty why
     I do what I happen to be doing. Sorrow comes
And takes you in its hand and then you can forget what the day was supposed
     to comprise and just follow its lead
Into the long shadows. The other days it's up to you to choose.
     Why not follow that friend of a friend
Of my brother's who stopped his car at the center of the George Washington Bridge
     just yesterday afternoon and climbed
Over the rail? I heard this on the phone today. He'd been a diver at Yale
     so when he dove he must have cut the air
In a straightening arc with grace enough to banish chaos until he hit.
     That the surface of the river
Would be pulled tighter than he'd ever tried is a thing he must have known.
     What everyone is saying is that he didn't

Seem depressed. Why not follow him then? No thanks, I'd rather live some more
    than tatter myself against the water or pluck a nightshade
Berry to eat or wind up folded into the wreckage of my brother's car. No reason why.
    I would, that's all. Without me I'm nothing.
Maybe I'll learn to drive and get my own car. Maybe I can buy the diver's car
    if it survived. What he'd have wanted
For it won't be known, but who knows, maybe my brother can tell me more,
    there may be more to this than meets the eye. I'll see.
One more girl blades by better looking than the rest and kinder no doubt, wiser
    no doubt, though there's no time to find that out
As the aforementioned Porsche pulls up and the heart lifts in its cheap, real, momentary
    gladdening, the massage of privilege, and I'm watched
By her now so that there's an instant where I'm aloft in someone else's dream
    and I forget that I've been found
With my arms on my knees and my legs asleep, asway a bit, in a trance, almost,
    from watching spring fly by too slow to notice
And the girls so long in bloom so that it couldn't matter less that I've been waiting.

Christopher Cahill lives in New York City,
where he was born. His novel, Perfection,
was published in Paris by L'Age d'Homme.